# The Dead Spirits at the Piano

# The Dead Spirits at the Piano

Poems by Carol Jennings

Cherry Grove Collections

© 2016  by Carol Jennings

Published by Cherry Grove Collections
P.O. Box 541106
Cincinnati, OH 45254-1106

ISBN: 9781625491794

Poetry Editor: Kevin Walzer
Business Editor: Lori Jareo

Visit us on the web at www.cherry-grove.com


Cover photograph by Joseph Llobrera

# Acknowledgments

With gratitude to the editors of the journals and anthologies where some of the poems in this collection previously appeared:

"*Mano Sinistra*": *Chautauqua,* Issue 11, 2014; winner of the 2013 Chautauqua Institution Mary Jean Irion Poetry Prize

"In Rome with John Keats": *The Broadkill Review,* March/April 2015

"Playing Debussy": *The Broadkill Review,* March/April 2015

"Epistle to Paul from the Ruins of Ephesus": *The Broadkill Review,* March/April 2015

"The Dead Composers": *Innisfree Poetry Journal*, Vol. 16, Spring 2013

"The Color of Voice": *Medical Literary Messenger,* Vol. 2, No. 2, Spring 2015

"Sonnet for the Dead": *Oberon*, second annual issue, 2003

"Love Letter to Chopin": *Chopin with Cherries: A Tribute in Verse*, ed. by Maja Trochimczyk, Moonrise Press 2010

"Emily": *Potomac Review,* Vol. VII, No. 1, Winter 1999-2000; reprinted in *Canadian Woman Studies/les cahiers de la femme* (York University, Toronto) Vol. 20, No. 3, Fall 2000

"Office Suicide": *Beltway Poetry Quarterly,* Vol. 13:3, Summer 2012

"Dysthymia": *Chautauqua,* Issue 6, 2009; winner of the 2008 Chautauqua Institution Poetry Contest

"The Other": *Oberon,* second annual issue, 2003

"The Train from Guangzhou to Beijing": *Journeys Along the Silk Road* (Lost Tower Publications, London) 2015

"Shanghai": *Amelia,* Vol. VII, No. 3, 1994

"The Burren": *The Broadkill Review,* March/April 2015


With thanks to David and Lisa for their ongoing support.

And much gratitude to Elisavietta Ritchie, David Keplinger, and the late William Packard, the best mentors a poet could have.

*I have walked through many lives,*
*some of them my own,*
*and I am not who I was,*

    Stanley Kunitz, "The Layers," *Passing Through*


    *if I could know*
*in what language to address*
*the spirits that claim a place*

    Adrienne Rich, "Toward the Solstice,"
*The Dream of a Common Language*


and you
cold universe
sustain me

    William Packard, *voices/I hear/voices*

*for my brother, Alan Booth, 1935-2015*

*Table of Contents*

## I. Speaking with Spirits

| | |
|---|---|
| *Mano Sinistra*..................................................................................17 | |
| In Rome with John Keats............................................................19 | |
| Playing Debussy............................................................................21 | |
| Epistle to Paul from the Ruins of Ephesus ............................23 | |
| The Dead Composers....................................................................25 | |
| My Mother's Piano........................................................................27 | |
| Counting Mozart............................................................................29 | |
| With Liszt At the Piano ..............................................................31 | |
| The Color of Voice .......................................................................33 | |
| Sonnet for The Dead.....................................................................35 | |
| Love Letter to Chopin..................................................................36 | |
| Emily................................................................................................38 | |
| Mahler's Symphony No. 2 in C Minor: *Resurrection*...............40 | |
| With Grieg In Fjord Country.....................................................42 | |
| St. Francis Tends the Hearts......................................................44 | |
| Elegy for a Poet ............................................................................46 | |
| The Druggist's Daughter............................................................48 | |
| The Sun Shall Not Strike You by Day, Nor the Moon by Night............................................................................50 | |
| My Mother's Voice........................................................................51 | |

## II. If Any Lover

If Any Lover....................................................................................55
Dust Jacket......................................................................................57
Death of the First Lover...............................................................58

Little Red Riding Hood.................................................................60
Villanelle for the Lover's Return ................................................62
Class Reunion................................................................................63
Love for One Season....................................................................64
Across Lake Willoughby..............................................................65
When an Old Lover Dies..............................................................67
Oysters............................................................................................68

## III. Notes to the Suicides

Office Suicide................................................................................73
Grandmother Carrie.....................................................................75
The Whale Beaches Herself.........................................................77
On the Metro with Sylvia & Ted ................................................79
Ophelia to Hamlet........................................................................81
Death by Subway..........................................................................83

## IV. The Demons Come out of the Dark

Dysthymia .....................................................................................87
Dreams of a Common Dark........................................................90
*Diminuendo*....................................................................................91
The Art of the Scalpel...................................................................93
The Other.......................................................................................95
In This Pink Room........................................................................97
The Queen of Hearts.....................................................................99
Aurora...........................................................................................100
Cross Country..............................................................................102
Bedtime for Insomniacs .............................................................103
The Separated Self .....................................................................105
Mother at 91.................................................................................107
Sunday Rites ...............................................................................108

# V. Solstice to Equinox

Summer Solstice .................................................................... 111
August Heat Wave................................................................. 112
Tamarack Tree....................................................................... 114
Autumn Equinox................................................................... 115
Woman in Thin October Light ........................................... 117
The Train from Guangzhou to Beijing (1979)................... 118
Shanghai (1978)..................................................................... 120
November.............................................................................. 122
Flu........................................................................................... 123
Winter Solstice...................................................................... 124
New Year's Eve..................................................................... 125
Twelfth Night........................................................................ 126
Weather Report..................................................................... 128
Turning Sixty........................................................................ 129
Vernal Equinox..................................................................... 131
Late Snow.............................................................................. 132
Spring Cleansing ................................................................. 133
Salmon Run........................................................................... 134
Athabasca.............................................................................. 136
The Burren............................................................................ 137
Nebulae.................................................................................. 138

# I. Speaking with Spirits

## Mano Sinistra

I have carried mother's tattered
Schubert sonatas, impromptus,
fantasias back and forth
to piano lessons. Bought
before I was born, binding
held by tape, its cover
and pages leave paper crumbs
on walkways, in cars, on pianos.
For months, I have struggled
with the B flat major Sonata,
composed two months before
his young death; its broad
reaches exceed mine, as I recall
how mother's long fingers
handled them with ease.
*Here*, my teacher says, *skip
to the Andante movement –
it's astounding, and you can do it.*
He shows me how it is played:
the left hand, *mano sinistra*,
crossing over the right to touch
the upper octave ever so lightly,
a sound you can barely hear
but feel that you have heard it.
As he plays, I hear mother
fifty years ago at her piano,
while in the next room,
I read, solved math problems,
daydreamed my future;
mother giving voice

to Schubert's sense of death,
me absorbing both of them,
but barely so, not knowing it.
I rush home to her piano,
now mine,
so we can play Schubert,
mourn him a little,
the two of us, together.

# In Rome with John Keats

In the small room where you died,
I stand at the end of a narrow bed,
as perhaps you did on better days,
stare out the window at Bernini's boat
still sinking on the Piazza di Spagna.

And had you not been so weak,
his marble boat, like the Elgin Marbles,
might have sparked another ode or sonnet
on mortality – a new metaphor
for the life slowly leaving you.

In those last days, to which poem
did you turn for comfort?
I would guess the Nightingale –
your darkling singing to you
in full throated summer ecstasy

out of the embalming dark, in high
requiem for a coming February death.
Or could it be the urn? – with lovers
on the brink, like you and Fanny,
bliss always out of reach.

Nothing is left of your time here
but Severn's death-bed portrait –
tendrils of hair damp on your forehead,
lids shut, candles throwing shadows
on your face, still perfect at the end.

Though they burned all you touched,
in a bonfire below, you linger here listening
for footsteps on the stairs, horses on the square,
mandolin players on the Spanish steps,
the poem in the blood rising in your throat.

# Playing Debussy

She spun notes for you
in her wistful way,
the girl with the flaxen hair.

I was that girl in a younger self,
playing you in the key of G flat,
fingers always light as you desired.

I have more years now than you
at death, and find you less mystical
than I did when I was her.

I still love it when your major and minor thirds
roll off my fingertips; I marvel
that the dramas of your life –

affairs with Parisian ladies,
the wife who shot herself but lived,
wars that roared through France,

cancer that consumed you –
these stories are not replayed
in the soft refraction of your scores.

You hated the word *impressionist*,
yet blurred your tones
as the painters their colors and lines.

Though I have left behind
the flaxen-haired girl,
I have not given you up.

The ephemeral light of your moon
still splays across my piano keys,
prevents me from sleeping.

The floating chords of your sunken
cathedral, *La Cathedrale Engloutie*,
mimic the rise and fall of tides –

a stretch for small hands, stiff fingers;
yet, I want to bring the illusion
out of the water for you, again.

# Epistle to Paul from the Ruins of Ephesus

I see you stalk
these marble streets
in anger, hear you harangue
silversmiths, harlots,
worshippers descending temple steps.

It was not, you know,
about the gospel you preached,
or your fabled vision
on the Damascus road,

but only about the art
you wanted to kill –
their silver statues of Goddess
of childbirth, the hunt and the moon,
Artemis, molded so delicately,
with testicles of bulls
in place of her breasts.

You believe this city deserved
its fate – assault by Goths
who wrecked her temple
save a single marble column,
then slow death as the seaport
silted over, blocked ships bearing
oil, saffron, silk, purple dye
from the mucus of mollusks.

But, did you see what brings us back
to this place, even in ruins?
Though you surely eschewed
the temples and brothel,
did you pause from argument
to admire Hercules' Gate,
Aphrodite's statue, or
the marble Arcadian Way
from harbor to amphitheater? –
where they put you on trial,
ordered you out of town.

I re-read your letter to Ephesians.
Though eloquent on love and grace,
dark and light, faith and unity,
you were too heavy-handed
with admonitions –

> *don't drink too much wine,*
> *wives submit to husbands*
> *(as though you knew of marriage),*
> *children obey parents,*
> *slaves obey masters,*
> *pray at all times –*
> *especially for the saints and for you –*

already convinced
you were destined
to be one of them.

# The Dead Composers

Evenings they keep company
with me.  I begin with Mozart,
who flits about the room,
glass of wine in hand, laughs
at my wrong notes or slips of rhythm,
tells a dirty joke when I pause
between parts.  I want to play him
with elegance, share supper with him,
save him from that early death.

But I can do none of these,
so on to Beethoven's *Pathetique*.
I love him best for pouring
light and dark into every score –
though now he glowers in the corner,
does not forgive mistakes,
never smiles, even if well played.

It gets late, so I shift to romantics,
who impatiently wait their turns.
Chopin wrote nocturnes for married women –
were they patrons or lovers, I boldly ask?
He smiles mysteriously, does not reply.

Liszt wrote for hands larger than mine
changes key often, complicates the rhythm;
yet he allows for liberties,
as Mozart never will,
and I am grateful to him for that.

I like to close with Brahms,
who dreamed, I'm sure, of holding Clara
through his waltzes and rhapsodies.
But Schumann frowns at me from the stairs,
so I mollify him with *Scenes of Childhood*.
Schubert must wait until tomorrow.

Like having multiple lovers –
these connections
of cadences and keys,
chords and accidentals,
changing tempos,
touches of ivory, not flesh.

They are faithful in their way,
the dead composers,
spirits who come
when summoned by their notes,
but always know it's time to leave
as I close the keyboard lid,
dim the overhead light.

# My Mother's Piano

At the end of her life,
it could not hold a tune –
just as the neurons of her brain
could not hold a memory
of what happened yesterday.

When people around her left home,
died or disappointed her,
the piano was always there –
offering the cool touch of ivory,
the comfort of Schubert and Chopin.

After she died,
piano movers removed its legs,
slid it sideways out the front door,
down the brick steps,
out of her reach forever.

I dismantled her life – unsealed papers,
sold furniture, gave away paintings –
while others dismembered the piano,
removed strings, hammers, dampers,
pedals, cracked soundboard,

then put it back together
with new taut steel wires
and red felted hammers,
ivory keys capped like old teeth,
mahogany case sanded, stained.

I have made it mine –
its dark luster dominates
my living room, my evenings,
tempers my restlessness,
smooths passage to another decade.

Mother is with me as I play,
sits next to me on the bench,
hovers over the raised lid,
or flutters at my back
in that flighty way of the dead.

I play from sheet music
decomposing at the edges,
her neat pencil marks still visible
over and under the staff.
Even in death, she corrects

my wrong notes, lapses in tempo,
inappropriate fortés.
I pay attention to her,
more than when she was alive.
In the spirit world, she is with the Romantics;
they may whisper to her of true intent.

# Counting Mozart

With you, it's always about the rhythm.
When the notes are almost there, and
the turns roll off my fingers like sand,
it's counting you that makes me stumble.

Did you drive Constanze crazy with your need
for perfect balance in each *motif*, never rushing
a conclusion, never lingering in the middle
over a sweet phrase or silky touch?

If you had lived to be old,
perhaps you would have let go
of your classical precision,
permitted a few romantic liberties,

a dalliance here or there,
rather than forcing us to borrow
time from one note to grace
another with flourish or trill.

Did you try to do this at the end
of your life – borrow time? –
a few more weeks, days, or even
hours, as your own requiem

coursed through your body
faster than your fingers scribbled,
holding back the end as though
death would wait for the music to stop.

I play your next to last piano sonata,
impatient for measure ten, a melodic
resolution so perfect it seems to answer
a question not yet asked.

I love you for it each time;
but a few bars later,
trip over you again.

# With Liszt At the Piano

So easily am I seduced
by your songs of consolation,
your numbered dreams of love.
Then just when I think
I can play you as you intended,
with even triplets,
the right measure of passion,
you complicate the rhythm,
score four notes in one hand
against three in the other,
demand long leaps of my left hand,
or change key suddenly –
five flats to four sharps,
accidentals tossed in
for dissonance before resolution.

You must have been that kind of lover,
demanding, hard to interpret, shifting
moods as often as key signatures.
And when a woman left,
what would you do?
Rhapsodize in a minor key,
compose a love theme
in broken chords,
rush the tempo
while waiting for her to return
as you knew she would? –

as I will because I can't abstain
for long.  Chopin makes me weep –
but practicing you, I fall in love again.

# The Color of Voice

Because my father lost
his larynx to cancer,
and my voice rasps

when I need it most,
the throat doctor slides
his strobe lit camera

down the back of my tongue
tied in white gauze
so as not to trip

this high-tech probe
into the origins
of my words.

Though I am drugged
on the palindrome of Xanax,
back of my mouth

numbed by a viscous gargle
and a spray that tastes of banana,
entry is not easy for him.

I dream of other substances
I did not want to swallow:
seawater and semen,

the flesh of lamb,
communion wafers,
bitter tonic I was forced

to drink as a child,
when my parents
thought me too thin.

Suddenly, I want to speak –
words I never said
when they were right:

*I don't love you;*
or *I'm not sorry;*
or *I can't stay with you.*

When I let go
for a moment,
the doctor has his picture,

then another.
Pleased, he steps back,
displays his photos –

the fuchsia flowers of my voice.
My throat is open again,
and silence returns.

# Sonnet for The Dead

Strange how they return to play
leading roles in dreams, or pass through a room
in daylight, look unchanged, and pause to say,
as they did before: *It's not as bad as you think.*
As though they cannot quite let go of you, or the life
where nothing is easy, except death.  As though
the new state is too ethereally flat and plain,
lacking the hard edges of conflict, choice.

Or do we have it all wrong?  Perhaps they drift, cirrus-
like and give us not a glance or thought, have blotted out
those of us still wrapped in skin, who check the time.
Have they cut us loose? – to replay their voices like favorite
sonatas, as we try to hold them in relationships with a name,
that are bound by blood, as though the blood still flowed.

# Love Letter to Chopin

At thirteen, I fell in love with you,
upon hearing the Nocturne in E flat,
and practiced for five years
to play you with the right *legato* and *rubato*,
trusting you would listen from some
heavenly perch and send me
a sign of your approval. It never came,
so I moved on to Liszt, with whom
you also shared lovers, I have read.

I wonder about Camilla –
pianist, married to a piano maker,
three of your Nocturnes dedicated to her.
But did you love her and she you?
And did you tell her in words
or only through the melody?
For me, it would have been enough.

And the other women,
married, unmarried,
countesses, princesses,
to whom you dedicated
waltzes, ballades, mazurkas, etudes –

were they lovers and muses,
or just pianists with the right touch?
And what about George Sand –
the love of your life, biographers write,
yet nothing is dedicated to her?

I have come back to you years later,
not with the passion of adolescence,
but the sensibilities of an older woman,
and a willingness to take romantic liberties.

# Emily

> *My life closed twice before its close —*
> *It yet remains to see*
> *If Immortality unveil*
> *A third event to me*
>                 Emily Dickinson

How do you feel
about tourists traipsing
through your house
each hour of the afternoon,
standing, silent, around your bed
as though you linger here,

might impart one more
metaphor or rhyme,
a line or two on the after death,
name someone you love, or
tell if your view of God has changed.

Poems you left in a box,
now laminated in plastic,
pass, hand to hand.

Alive today, you would like
the freedom of verse,
but not the critics,
rejection slips,
writers conferences,
casual sexual encounters.

Would you take a lover,
swallow Prozac,
watch television,
give readings,
enter therapy?

Or would you stay within yourself,
in the house of your birth,
ignore the phone,
retreat to your room,
hide poems under the bed,
wait for life to close
three times and then again.

# Mahler's Symphony No. 2 in C Minor: *Resurrection*

> *You are battered to the ground*
> *with clubs and then lifted to the heights on*
> *angels' wings.*
>                 Mahler to Bruno Walter, 1900

You scored your whole life
in the first two symphonies –
and when you reached the final
chorus of *Aufersteh'n*,
was it vision of your own death
that propelled you
measure by measure?

Or the coffins of all those children
who preceded you
through the gate to the grave,
for whom you wished
the heights of angels' wings?

And what kept you going
to Number Nine and part of Ten?
having orchestrated death so well
with mixed choir, E-flat clarinets,
two sets of timpani, contrabassoons,
cymbals, glockenspiel.

Did you think it might come again,
the epiphany?

Or was it all that separated you
from your dark, Bohemian side,
from the abyss,
where the Bird of Death
trilled her siren song,

where you knew
you would not return
if you walked too near.

# With Grieg In Fjord Country

I did not come to Norway looking for you,
but you are everywhere, your A Minor
Concerto pulsating with the hairpin loops
of our bus high above the fjords.

The notes of your lyric themes
were shaped in these glacier-carved
waters, deeper than most imaginations,
mirror for mountains always under snow,

while your *Peer Gynt* suite was spun
out of the forest where trolls and gnomes
stormed from the Hall of the Mountain King
across your piano keys.

You laughed at your own music for its very
Norwegian-ness, called it the taste of codfish,
the odor of cow dung in the pasture,
too full of *trollish self-satisfaction*.

At the Lofthus inn where you stayed in summer,
you stand carved in wood in the garden
by the cottage where you composed
at a piano no longer played, long out of tune.

Surprised by your small stature,
I put my arm around you, though
your wife, also in wood, stands close behind.
I never imagined you a short man.

At the hotel in Bergen,
where you collapsed before dying,
I wander the hallways at night –
your ghost lingers here,

also at *Troldhaugen*,
your villa outside of town, now
a tourist stop, as you may observe
from the cliff-side grotto where they buried

both of you.  I pause at your back door
to have my photo shot while absorbing
the lake view, happy for you
that Norway loved you and you lived well.

Home again at my own piano, I play
*The Last Spring* every day, try to plumb
this unexplained elegy that caused
Tchaikovsky to weep, now me as well.

I like that you felt no need to explain
its sadness, played out with a touch
that does not overwhelm, but brushes
lightly, a bit of mystery in its sense of ending.

# St. Francis Tends the Hearts

In the heart hospital hall,
visitors step
on dusty-pink hearts
appliquéd to gray tiles.

These cut-outs remind
patients in bathrobes
why they are here;
mark boundaries
of electronic tether
to wireless monitor
that measures every beat,
pause, arrhythmic flutter.

We ask so much of this hollow
organ with its four small rooms.
Designed only to pump blood,
it is also expected
to recognize the right partner,
generate a life span of love,
forgive wrongs to its owner,
supply courage on demand,
all this while thumping along,
not too loudly.

As we say goodbye
to our sister and cross
the plastic perimeter of hearts,
my own seems to jump a little.

St. Francis stands
in stone at the entrance –
in passing I ask
that he please keep us
in rhythm a while longer.

# Elegy for a Poet

Before we lost touch,
we shared metaphors,
pool-side talk of Paris,
tales of ex-lovers, especially
the one we had in common.
Years later, I looked for you
at his funeral, surprised
you were not there.

I searched your name
on the Internet to find
perhaps a poem,
collection, essay on craft;
what I found was a photo
of a southern gravestone,
the epitaph:
"Her spirit is truly free".

Like him, you died too soon,
leaving only questions: why
you traded New York for Tennessee;
why there is no book of you;
why your spirit was not free enough
in your body; whether you died
by choice.

With no one to ask – I look
to your early poems, those lines like:

*her tongue*
*is an animal*
*caught in a trap*

*it writhes at the root*
*of his silence*

Neither of us could write elegies;
so I re-arrange your lines,
steal a few similes,
try to swallow your voice.

Italicized lines from: Linda Krenis, "The Quarrel," *The New York Quarterly*, No. 1, Winter 1970.

# The Druggist's Daughter

The blue bottle in the back
room of the antique shop –
cork pushed inside, by itself
amidst a sea of old green glass –
takes me back. Through
its cobalt translucence, I glimpse
my father filling prescriptions
at the corner of Hamlin and Main,
behind a tall counter adorned
only by a sign with his name
and another blue bottle,
next to a cork press, symbols
of an earlier time in apothecaries
when pharmacists mixed powders
and liquid potions, pressed corks
to fit bottles, blue, green, or clear.
He was fond of that history.

I see myself too,
behind the front counter,
as I ring up sales, wonder
about the lives of people
buying pain relief,
bandages, lipstick, face cream.
Men who seek condoms
do not look me in the eye,
ask to speak to my father.
I want to ask them why
they do not leave this town,
to me so empty and small.

When business is slow,
I take out a book, Salinger
or Fitzgerald, though Father
disapproves my reading fiction
in full view of any customer
walking through the door,
suggests I dust shelves instead.

I like the way he looks
in his druggist jacket of white or blue,
like to watch him count and measure
behind the blue bottle and cork press;
at home we argue, often in raised voices,
about my late night hours,
the boys whose company I favor.

I take the bottle home
for my blue-tiled bathroom,
set it on the marble shelf between
the elegant blue bottle from Prague,
hand painted with white flowers,
and a mottled blue oblong of blown
glass from Oregon. I see them
morning and evening,
glass blues of my life.

# The Sun Shall Not Strike You by Day, Nor the Moon by Night

*Psalm 121: 6*

April snow falls fast, unexpected.
In the sanctuary, we say a psalm in unison,
lift our eyes to the hills,
    though none are visible,
give death a voice.
*We see through a glass darkly*, we are told.

The congregation sings *Come Down O Love Divine*.
The handbell choir rings full, sad notes.
Brahms, Beethoven, Bach impose
    their visions of order and clarity.
We praise her strength of will,
determination – now a force beyond
the pull of gravity.

Then, we leave this crush of music and words,
slog in silence through snow,
still restless
as the last spring storm subsides.
Now we turn to the real tasks:
    divide her things,
    dismantle her life.

This is what she wanted –
she is untethered,
a lacuna in my life.
The sun shall not strike her by day,
nor the moon by night.

# My Mother's Voice

The voices of dead lovers
come to me only in the dark,
hours when I should be asleep.
But my Mother's voice is heard
late afternoons in autumn
or very early spring.
The sun is low in the sky.
Chill seeps in through cracks
in the windows.
As I close the piano lid,
half notes linger in the room.

## II. If Any Lover

# If Any Lover

If any lover were to come back
from the dead,
it would have to be you.

*But I didn't really die,*
you say, *I staged a death
to marry Sofia.*

*Who is Sofia?* I ask.
*She is the one
I wanted you to be.*

You stand there in a half light,
wearing white and black,
as you did when we were young.

My arms circle you
as they often have
in pre-dawn dreams.

I decide: I will come
with you to Prague,
tell no one you are alive.

You almost smile,
as in the photo I have
of you at seventeen.

I arrange a passport in Sofia's name,
pack a few summer clothes,
paisley skirt, white shawl.

When I look for you again,
you are not there – it was
always that way with you.

Grandmother warned:
> *Be careful whom you love at seventeen,*
> *he will have a death grip on your life.*

# Dust Jacket

Browsing at Kramer Books
and Afterwords,
my fingers catch
your latest work.
I pull you from the shelf;
your dust-jacket
stare startles me
as it did decades ago.
I have to take you home,
as I did then, though
I no longer need
your body or affection,
just your words in hard-cover edition,
a space for you in the oak bookcase
between Rilke's *Letters to a Young Poet*
and Jong's *Fear of Flying*.

# Death of the First Lover

You knew all the places
we would not be discovered –
abandoned shack in the woods,
hidden loft above the garage,
grassy patch by a stream,
a house half built.

Sex with you was a dusty affair,
and afterwards you always wanted
to talk about something
complex but elegant,
like nuclear fusion.

For me, you were Keats' negative capability –
a *beauty is truth and truth beauty*
kind of romantic, with a steel-edged mind.
At eighteen I was in love with you both.

I predicted your early death,
in April with everything on the verge.
You were careless with chemicals,
with electricity, and, yes, even with love.
You could have died in a thousand ways,

and the press clip – posted by mother,
who never liked you – does not disclose
which one or whether it was a method
of your own choosing. I cannot wrap
my arms around your new status.

But obituaries don't tell true stories.
Your wife disconnected the phone,
left town suddenly.
You're as much a mystery dead
as you were alive.
You wrote this ending.

# Little Red Riding Hood

She ignored her mother's warning:
> *Take the basket straight to grandmother's,*
> *don't loll in the forest, don't talk to strangers.*

In the sparkling summer noon,
she picked flowers, stopped
to chat with that rakish wolf
who sidled up to her, asked questions.

By the time she reached her grandmother's,
the wolf had broken the flimsy door,
scared the old lady into a closet,
dressed himself in a lace negligee.

Riding Hood played coy, commented
on his ears, eyes, mouth, other body parts,
until he chased her around the bed,
pounced and devoured her whole.

Tired by all this cavorting, the wolf slept
until a kindly hunter who happened by
sized up the situation and slit his belly,
like a surgeon performing C-section.

Red Riding Hood set free,
he filled the empty belly with rocks
to cure the wolf's penchant for little girls,
sewed him up, sent him into the woods.

Grandmother came out of the closet,
and all three (famished by trauma)
lunched on the picnic – French bread,
grapes, brie, chocolate cake.

They all lived happily ever after;
Red Riding Hood always did
her mother's bidding,
or so the story goes . . .

But I know better,
having met a few
wolves in disguise:
she still dons red velvet,

slips now and then into the forest
to meet the brawny hunter,
who is the daddy she never had,
or to play kinky games with the wolf,

who wasn't fooled by the stones;
and when grandmother travels abroad,
girl, hunter, and wolf meet at the cottage
to play their fantasies once again.

# Villanelle for the Lover's Return

When the lover returns, it will be in a dream
His time in your life comes always too late
At the edges of light, things are not what they seem

Love slices sudden, sharp, a carnal scream
It is never right, though it may seem like fate
When the lover returns, it will be in a dream

You are dazzled and manic, clouded as cream
Wild in your reach, you do not hesitate
At the edges of light, things are not what they seem

You unclasp your hair, you are caught in the beam
You dance in purple, circle desire inchoate
When the lover returns, it will be in a dream

Loss comes as suddenly as frost kills green
The unraveling is slow, and so you wait
At the edges of light, things are not what they seem

Alone, you rewrite the affair, alter the scenes
The end of the story is yours to create
When the lover returns, it will be in a dream
At the edges of light, things are not what they seem

# Class Reunion

From the edge of my eye,
I think I glimpse you,
then hear your voice
cut the crowd behind me;
some time this night
your dark stare
will trap me again.
I delay the moment
as long as I can,
though when it happens
I am no less surprised.

We stand close,
do not touch.
*If you could will everyone else
to disappear right now, would you?*
you ask, and I whisper *yes*.
You were the first for me,
and that love has no past tense.
As always with you,
I dance with the devil.

Other old loves press close;
your wife hovers nearby.
We talk of time, drift apart,
pretend indifference.
Later I look for you,
but you are gone –
it always happened that way.

# Love for One Season

What began in February
with a long look,
a brush of hands
in an empty loft
under exposed beams,
fading light folded
into the pitch of roof,

by the longest day of the year,
was stretched brittle thin,
and there was no other way
than to leave you suddenly.

I exorcised you
in one night:
changed numbers, locks,
burned messages,
poured wine down the drain,
deleted dreams.

For all of the heat,
we were never right.

# Across Lake Willoughby

Light cuts black water with a moon-gold knife.

This August night
we could be seventeen,
when hands groped
uncertain under cotton folds.

Love was the only urgency,
time elongated
like this glacier-
gouged lake,

marriages, children
a far landscape,
death unconsidered
as a distant winter.

Headlights intrude,
skim the ripples;
a car door slams.
We are no longer seventeen,

and know too well
the borders of our lives.
Nothing to do but
follow a trail back

to dim porch lights,
voices swirled with crushed
ice, rum & lime,
intoxicating.

Behind us, laughter
from our former selves
planes the lake,
thin, black pebbles.

# When an Old Lover Dies

When an old lover dies, he takes
the part of me that danced over quicksand.

When an old lover dies, he crushes
a cigarette on the tight skin of early years.

When an old lover dies, a former self
drops from peripheral vision.

When an old lover dies, my heart
admits to losing its rhythm.

When an old lover dies, he re-aligns
the margins of my life.

When an old lover dies, he haunts
a few more nights than I allotted him.

I like to think of them out there,
remembering slices of affairs –

half cups of espresso, hours by train,
short nights of edgy love,

words across the table, words
in blue-black ink, never words that held.

When an old lover dies, he leaves me
again – even if I did the leaving before.

# Oysters

*I am aware it is not good to eat oatmeal alone.
Its consistency is such that it is better for your mental health if
somebody eats it with you.*
        Galway Kinnell, "Oatmeal,"
        *When One Has Lived A Long Time Alone*

Even if you don't believe
the aphrodisiac myth,
you should not eat oysters alone.

Galway Kinnell warns against
spooning oatmeal in solitude –
invites dead poets to sit with him,

drive any dark spirits
from the breakfast table.
Yet he is silent on shellfish.

Does a bowl of lumpy oats
warrant more caution
than this creature live

on its open shell, dredged
from a shallow bay, bedded
on ice, acidic with lemon?

An imagined companion – even one
accomplished in music or letters
of another century – is not enough

to overcome the idea of the oyster
with its slippery little heart,
stomach, mouth, mantle, gills.

To swallow whole is a carnal act,
should not be performed in solitude –
a stranger at table will suffice,

even one who says he could not do
what you are doing, though not
opposed to watching it done.

Baked or fried – coated in crumbs
or chopped spinach and Parmesan –
you might get away with it and no regrets.

In a raw state,
even with oyster crackers on the side,
the danger signs are all around.

# III. Notes to the Suicides

# Office Suicide

So unlike you to leave early,
unfinished work a trail across the desk,
glasses perched on top hiding your intent
not to return.

Next morning, your computer blinks
the arrival of messages of no consequence
now that you've shot yourself in the head.

Your note at home was so like you –
explained nothing but site:
>*I'm under the deck,*
>*don't look, call for help.*

Weeks pass, we still linger
outside your open door –
as though you're connected
to this place, might suddenly appear,
demand to know what we are doing.

Our funereal tones of those first days
when death was fresh –
an avalanche, a tidal wave –
metamorphosed into chips
of obsidian humor: *Well at least*
*he didn't do it at work.*

Do you suicides congregate
in some otherworldly space,
chat about pros and cons –
oven, river, gun, pills, knife,
a leap, a rope, asphyxiation?
You would have weighed options.

I've adopted your philodendron,
twisted, overgrown,
pruned its stalk.
You called it a phoenix, invulnerable –
unlike you.

# Grandmother Carrie

You told stories of the farm in Ohio –
the day in August under the cherry tree,
you, sister Laura, and baby Libby,
rabid dog, foam at his mouth, lurching slowly
toward you. Laura shouted at you to climb
the tree, passed baby to you, then swung herself
up – just before the dog reached the blanket
where you had played moments before, tore into
the rag doll left behind, spit it out, swaggered
into direct aim of a neighbor's shotgun.
You spun these events as if ordinary, one
hot afternoon's adventure, did not mention fear.

Or the night your brother Ben returned from town
in a pony cart through sudden thunderstorm,
a wall of rain. Though the pony knew the way,
he turned too soon at the gate, stumbled in flooded
ditch, got caught in barbed wire fence; legs thrashed
wild in fear. Ben cut hands, arms trying to free him
until his brothers in the farmhouse heard cries,
rescued both and cleaned all lacerations.

I loved these stories of bad things that ended well –
you had lived the childhood of my storybooks.
Then when I was twelve, you put a knife to your throat
one cold Sunday afternoon in December.
What was in your mind that day? –
Did you think of the cherry tree and mad dog,
your doll between its teeth, or of big sister
Laura, who saved you all, or of brother Ben,

bloody hands trying in vain to untangle
pony from barbed wire?

Or was it something darker
in a place no one else knew,
beyond the farm boundary?
Though you survived that day,
I knew it was the end
of stories that ended well.

# The Whale Beaches Herself

> *I don't think two people could have been*
> *happier than we have been.*
> Virginia Woolf's note to Leonard
> before she walked into the river,
> March 28, 1941.

Was it a lyric voice
in the inner ear
that summoned you
from the sea?

Or a cacophony,
like the noise
that drove Virginia Woolf
into the water
a stone in her coat pocket
to ensure she did not fail
in this one episode
she would never describe.

Did it summon you
in your own language?
Or something strange
and human, you could not
understand or resist?

Did you leave a mate undersea,
and did you sing to him
before you swam aground,
of contentment
in the cold comfort
of ocean current.

# On the Metro with Sylvia & Ted

> *Now I drink from your stillness that neither*
> *Of us can disturb or escape.*
>     Ted Hughes, "Drawing,"
>     *Birthday Letters*

Mornings on the metro,
I mark minutes sifting
Ted's birthday poems to Sylvia.

Decades after her gas-jet death,
they fall from the page,
petals of an early dogwood
severed in a sudden
April downdraft.

Ted trying to save Sylvia
from the bell jar, the panic bird,
the bears, the Badlands,
snakes, cave bats,
careless poets,
her fever, her father,
her husband, herself.

Ted at the open coffin,
trying to save the rest
of his life from her.

Portrait of a marriage
from the manual
on marriages to avoid:
> *do not marry your own craziness;*
> *do not marry your muse;*
> *most of all, do not marry*
> *the one you think can save you.*

# Ophelia to Hamlet

If I could choose,
I would love Horatio,
a prince by nature
not by birth.
He would not
have thrust a rapier
through my father,
or any hidden fool.

Horatio is constant
as summer solstice light,
the long day that frees
winter-logged spirits.
You change as often
as the North Sea,
hammer those you love
like waves against rocks.

But, I am a girl
who teases death,
damned for loving
your sullen,
broody kind,
the bad boy of Elsinore,
prince of dark,
my father's murderer.

All my sins remembered,
I offer you fennel,
rosemary and rue,

take leave to follow
father and mother
to that undiscovered
country you fear too much.

# Death by Subway

Anna Karenina style –
a leap on the tracks,
a high speed train,
rush hour for extra drama.

Commuters throng
into the streets above,
wait for buses
that never come,

grumble about
the chaos of it all,
the inconvenience
of suicide.

*IV. The Demons Come out of the Dark*

# Dysthymia

Dressed in black
like a stagehand,
soft and swift
you alter sets in the dark,
pretend to be unnoticed,
know every move counts.

You hide
in closets, attics, cellars,
the synapses of my brain,
always ahead of me,
preparing the next
change of scene.

You were grandmother's
unwanted lover,
the lodger who left knives
within reach
on dreary winter days
in her old age.

You conspired,
when I was four,
with the crazy lady next door:
*That little girl is a bad one,*
you chanted in her ear,
*threaten to cut off her head.*
*It will frighten her away*
*until you are dead.*

You settled in for months
when I was twelve.
Friends, in ponytails
and plaid flannel,
closed me out of their circle.
*Pay no heed*
*they don't like you, but*
*you'll always have me.*

I once swallowed God
as an antidote, tried
to wrap myself
in a white light
you could not permeate.
You sulked, undaunted,
in a corner, waited
for the first cloud of doubt.

I've taken husbands, lovers
to keep you at bay.
But you are not
the jealous type. A cat,
you curl between the sheets,
where passion settles
like smoke: *See,*
*it can't last,* you hiss
in the aftermath.

The psychiatrist and I
talk you to death,
while you hover outside
in the coat closet.

When I slip my jacket
off the hangar, you mutter:
*Disparage me all you like
in the inner sanctum.
I'll wait. I'll have you again.*

# Dreams of a Common Dark

They come to me in a restless sleep,
grainy as old black and white films:

girl trapped in a hedgerow maze,
sparrow at the ceiling with no escape,

women of the demimonde with their marble lovers,
women who dress in black for all weathers,

the halls of Hamlet's castle
that empty one into the other,

the ghost of the father,
Gretel in the forest with no brother,

the poison hellebore,
an elevator stuck between floors,

communion of a mass suicide,
the airplane doomed before the dive,

unfinished sex in the wrong place
with a man who will not take off his clothes,

the car backing down a gravel drive
meets the blind spot in the mirror.

Morning comes, not too early.

## *Diminuendo*

> *Yet I could not bring myself to say to people:*
> *'Speak up, shout, for I am deaf.' Alas! how*
> *could I possibly refer to the impairing of a*
> *sense which in me should be more perfectly*
> *developed than in other people, a sense which*
> *at one time I possessed in the greatest perfection, . . . .*
> Ludwig Van Beethoven, letter to his brothers,
> 6 October 1802

At first, I blame the actors,
Shakespeare, Elizabethan dialect –
a few lines sloughed off
here and there, then
falling more often,
drops from muffling clouds.

Next it happens at movies,
dialogue among art thieves
plotting a Monet theft
drowned in the jazz
beat of suspense.

The ear, nose, and throat doctor
does not console,
says the treble ranges,
consonants, are first to go.

I want to hear from Beethoven –
play the C Minor Sonata,
*adagio cantabile.*
What did you notice first –

loss of women's voices,
a muted piano,
the shepherd's flute
silent only for you?

When the cochlear waves
stopped singing notes to your brain,
and you heard the symphony
only in your head as it spun
the neural path to your fingers
filling in notes on a blank score,

from that silent dark,
where did you tap
*Ode to Joy?*

# The Art of the Scalpel

Inner landscape of my knee –
white spheres captured
on pencil-thin camera
threaded into fissure of flesh,
while I was drugged and dreamt
of striped fish and coral reefs.

"Before" pictures reveal
a tattered topography:
    tosses from horses,
    falls down stairs,
    stumbles on cracked walks,
    kneeling on stone surfaces
        in prayer or despair.

My surgeon displays his "After" photos –
    clean sculpture of cartilage,
    edges round, ragged
    fragments trimmed,
    meniscus tear mended,
    signs of age obliterated.

I admire his art, as he expects.
*What else can you cut from me?* I want to ask.
    *shards of unwanted memory,*
    *shrapnel of loves gone bad,*
    *or the cancer of self-doubt?*

But I have no more joints to fix –
so he dismisses me, proffers
his photos as parting gift –
      pretty moons luminous
      on black background,
      orthopedic purity,
      no blood no scars.

*Have a nice life,* he smiles and leaves.

# The Other

She needs disapproval,
the way I crave
sugar and caffeine.

I've tried to name her –
not a Biblical name
that suggests virtue;
something smoky and sultry
that rolls off the tongue
like Elana or Alexandra.

*I keep you young*, she whispers,
*important now that you
have reached a certain age.*
*Grow up*, I tell her,
*or I may have to kill you.*
*You can't*, she taunts,
*I'd take you with me.*

Over the years,
I've done away with her
favorite diversions –
raw oysters, red wine,
marijuana, cigarettes,
lovers she counted
on her fingers and toes.

She is most useful
locked in a sunny room
with plenty of bond paper

to scrawl confessional
metaphors and rhymes.

I can earn a living for both of us.
Left on her own,
she'd be a kept woman.

# In This Pink Room

Where I once smoked
in secret, wrote notes
to God, and conjured

a boy with a foreign look
who would trace the rise
of a breast, strum a stringed
instrument and sing me out
of the serpentine grasp
of this town, I am
stretched out again
on the narrow bed.

I still resemble that girl,
though now of an age
where the ringing in my head
is loud as the winged insects
chanting summer nights,
shrill outside

this pale-curtained window
I always left open
for that boy who never came
and made me search for years
in the dusk of distant cities.

Downstairs,
mother grows old,
and the girl knows
there will come a time

I no longer return
to this house.

She wraps herself
around me, whispers:
*Don't leave me here.*

# The Queen of Hearts

Mrs. Hemlock, my childhood demon, lived
next door, tended a garden of annuals and herbs.
Frizzy hair stood on end, bordered her sharp witch face,
frightened children who ran shortcut across her yard.
A trampled petunia evoked fury one day;
*Who did this?* her voice hissed.
My friend Billy pointed to me,
though we had not played near
her beds of pink and white.
>*If you ever set foot in my yard again,*
>*I'll cut off your head!*

Mother tried to reassure me:
*She doesn't mean it. She won't hurt you.*
I was not convinced.

Braver children still ventured across her yard,
while I took the long way around,
glancing back, protective hand at my throat.
Through childhood, I looked for her in closets,
under cellar stairs, in shadows of attic and garage,
behind trees on unlighted streets.

Years passed, Mrs. Hemlock dead, the house sold,
before I crossed that property line again,
a chill at the back of my neck.
Decades later, I still avoid petunia beds and shortcuts.
Her yard blooms with roses, a pool was added.
But returning, I see her still, behind a trellis,
shrill ghost chanting: *I'll get you, I'll get you yet.*

# Aurora

Too tall and skinny at eleven,
she prefers books
to softball or swimming pools,
pedals a bicycle
down streets with tree names:
Hickory, Linden, Elm.
July breezes tug
at her wheat fine hair,
her dream of living
in the south of France
with a bearded poet
who plays a mandolin,
sings ballads of love.

When parents call their children
home from tree house,
vacant lot or dry creek bed
to kitchen suppers of fried chicken,
sweet corn, tomatoes from the vine,
she is framed in a window seat
in her lavender room reading
*The Lady of the Lake.*

Later she walks down Willow Street
to her grandmother's house,
huddles on the front steps,
talks in low tones about leaving this town,
as the old woman folds her arms,
nods, half smiles, and fireflies blink
the onset of dark.

# Cross Country

In a Vermont village
where snow climbs so deep
it half curtains
first story windows,
we ski past town hall and library,
herringbone uphill into pine woods
tracked with snow ribbons.

*You are too stiff,* my lover yells,
and I want to cry because
I cannot keep pace with him
because the trail is too steep
because I am still afraid
of falling because here as a child
riding horseback through these woods,
I believed someday I could do
anything . . . .

Later, I rest on my skis
at the edge of the pines.  Below,
in late afternoon candescence,
a lone figure glides *adagio*
across the frosted lake.

In this place,
I am as far
from my life
as I can be.

# Bedtime for Insomniacs

Bolt the door against demons,
intruders, lost lovers.

Lower the thermostat,
avoid overheated dreams.

Turn the cat out to probe
the underside of night.

Put pens away, lock
the diary against entry.

Wash hands and face, purge
the mind of reason and light.

Flip switches, room by room,
on the day's detritus:

recycled news of murder, war,
court decrees, storms;

half-formed arguments,
unfinished messages;

dishes not cleared,
love undeclared.

Don't untangle lies, add
costs, or repent sins.

Tell the spirits of the dead to leave
through one window left open.

Or, if they must stay, to settle down,
stop fluttering, cease commenting

on the messiness of life.

# The Separated Self

For months she tried on
all former selves
she could drag
from the black waves.

This was necessary, he said,
before they came back on their own
to grab her out of the hazy film
of a dream with unmarked exits,

or in ordinary daylight, step
in front of the car she drives
down streets so familiar
she does not look for shadows on the curb.

She breathes each one back to life,
forty-five minutes at a time,
makes them sit up and tell
their subplot of the story:

the child who played with demons;
the teen, sullen and shy;
the girl who married for anger, not love;
the woman who loved too often and wrong.

The past selves do not
apologize; nor do they want
to own her again, or stay past
the allotted time.

Their words commingle,
like their dead skin cells
and dust from their shoes.
They seem to know their place

in this collective talk cure.
She begins to like their casual familiarity,
almost fails to realize
when it is time for everyone to leave.

# Mother at 91

She loses days,
cannot remember
to swallow pills
or pay the light bill,
which opera she attended
or who died last week.

But she cannot lose her sorrow
that the tall front pine fell
in last winter's storm,
that her great grandfather owned slaves,
that she was not her father's favorite,
that he borrowed a gun
and shot her cat
for biting his finger
to the bone.

# Sunday Rites

In the church of my childhood, I dip bread in unfermented liquid
of grapes, wish for sacrament with burning incense and real wine.

They replaced the stained glass scene of Christ, children and lambs
with a clear window pane, shutters angled to beam a cross of light.

When they speak of Christ's body, I imagine myself
    Mary Magdalene,
massaging his feet with olive oil and wiping them with her hair.

When, in mid prayer, the pastor says *old age is a blessing*,
mother, beside me in the hard, wooden pew, laughs out loud.

I try to count the random acts of selection, natural or otherwise,
that gave me to this species, gender, time, village, dark spirit.

Given all possible combinations of sperm and egg,
the chance of any of us being here is too small to measure.

Can God be given credit for any of this?
Blamed for sending too many prophets?
The organ toccata fades; mother still smiles to herself.

*V. Solstice to Equinox*

# Summer Solstice

This time of year, I used to burn
with solar induced mania;
now the longest day enfolds,
softly, like an older love.

The garden suffers from neglect:
the impulse to dig, prune, weed
has paled like an early romance
or words not written down in time.

I still measure pieces of the moon,
with the help of Debussy for whom
its light dripped in arpeggios
across keys when sun went down,

and Beethoven, whose funereal sonata
was named for moonlight,
not by him, but others who heard
light over water in his darker tones.

Voices from the past re-enter me,
ghost-like in the hazy sleep of short
nights; at sunrise, I separate words
from the living and the dead.

Solar magnets still pull
my body northward. I read
old letters, buy a ticket to fly
into midnight sun.

# August Heat Wave

*Until they think warm days will never cease,*
  *For Summer has o'er-brimm'd their clammy cells.*
    John Keats, To Autumn

We move slowly as if in sleep
edged by a vision of Venus
with her hot cliffs and lava plains.

On Earth, sand beaches bake,
prairie grass rolls in flame,
while back in your kitchen,
boiled water swells tea leaves,
with a mist that scalds
fevered skin, hot to touch
as the first-time lover.

This air flattens us,
like cut-out dough figures
left in the oven too long.
Our metal rings remember
their molten state.

Those who talk weather
for a living run dry of words.
The sex writer, languid
at his desk, watches
sweat glisten on the girl
he conjures in a scant black top.

We plan a trip far North,
research mean Fahrenheit
in Iceland, Lapland,
Newfoundland.

It ends as suddenly
as a love affair at seventeen;
a front moves through; hot air
dissipates like volcanic ash.
You reach for a sweater.
Autumn signals.
Venus was only a dream.

# Tamarack Tree

Looking for the last
tamarack, we traveled
unpaved Vermont roads,
dusty with summer's end.

An oddity, this larch –
conifer that sheds
yellow needles, the way
maples drop their leaves.

The Cree dried its wood
for snowshoes and poles;
plied the sinuous root
to bind canoes;

pressed bitter inner bark
to stanch blood, cure earache;
chewed resin for stomach ills
and melancholia.

We could use Cree
healing now,
as a sudden V of geese
streams like a bad omen.

The serrated edge of autumn
cuts the year;
what we looked for
last summer
eludes us still.

# Autumn Equinox

> *This thou perceiv'st, which makes thy love*
> *more strong,*
> *To love that well which thou must leave ere long.*
> William Shakespeare

This time of year,
Shakespeare looked
in his lover's eyes,
saw his own death.

You and I watch
children return to school,
faces sun-drenched
with summer,

even as October burns
rust, crimson, gold,
shades from boxes
of four dozen crayons.

Sad, this loss of light.
I want only to follow
the day to New Zealand
or Tasmania.

Instead we plant bulbs
and yellow mums,
rake leaves,
bake pumpkin bread,

shake blankets out of cedar,
try to love well
while waiting
for frost to kill.

# Woman in Thin October Light

She bleeds her hidden colors,
like the ash, willow, oak,
into margins of a year
gone bad with drought,
flood, earthquakes
along unexpected faults.

After equinox,
bones thin, skin sheds
as sun withdraws
from the hemisphere.
The body becomes
weightless as words.

She no longer sees
reflections in pool or mirror,
just something diaphanous,
without form or substance.
Rings are loose on her fingers;
she no longer walks, but floats
undefined, without edge.

She hovers, questions:
> *do I still exist?*
> *is this the only one I can be?* —

leans into the dark
of an Arctic night,
tries to slip into a body
more familiar,
perhaps an earlier life.

# The Train from Guangzhou to Beijing (1979)

From southern rice paddies
to northern coal dust,
for two nights and a day
on a crowded train,
we share a compartment
with a family –
the father going home to die
but unaware of his condition
states the Hong Kong doctor's
letter, written in English
that he cannot read,
but proudly shows us, the Americans.

His grown son and daughter
in People's Republic uniform blue
tuck their parents into lower berths,
spend the night on hard chairs
in the narrow corridor
(unable to pay for beds),
watch and listen as the old man's
body quakes with coughing
through the long nights.

The only Caucasians on the train,
my sister and I in our upper berths
play gin rummy and scrabble,
laugh like girls at camp.
For an hour in the afternoon,
we sit with the family
and watch farm workers,

who do not look up from the fields,
and children beside the track,
who wave us north,
and we all smile at each other
as we sip our flower tea,
having no common words.

## Shanghai (1978)

Her harbor throbs
with sampans, tugs and junks.
Garlic and ginger roll from carved doors
to her imperial mansions
crammed with proletarians, now.
Old men dance
in her streets at dawn,
and she is filled with boys
lured from collective farms
by her lights on the water,
her girls with curl in their hair,
red on their lips.
Sex thickens
in the old French quarter
and downtown alleys after dark.
She cannot quite purge
the barbarian ways.

A boy of sixteen falls into step
with me on the harbor walk.
>*Will you talk with me and*
>*may I buy you tea?* he asks.
>*How many rooms has your house in America,*
>*how much money do you earn,*
>*what do you think of my country,*
>*will you bear children someday?*

He takes my answers and recedes into streets
swelling with bicycles, sweat
and workers in quilted blue.
I take my parcels of silk
into the Peace Hotel for foreigners only.

# November

Gibbous moon hovers
among charcoal clouds.
Cats stalk their shadows.

Leaves crisp, prepare to fall.
Frost edges in, shrivels
the final vines.

A woman tightens her shawl.
This month chills,
divides.  Love ebbs.

We do not sign our work.
We leave in the dark.

# Flu

It strikes suddenly, like love,
in the midst of something ordinary:
washing a glass, wrapping a gift.
Joints are stunned with hurt,
the flesh prickles hot and cold,
not unlike a flash of desire
though touch is not welcome.

Fever brings a kind of calm;
there is no place to go,
no decision to be made,
no meal to prepare.
Plath's words in *Fever 103°*
become a mantra:
    *I am too pure for you or anyone.*
Ice water in easy reach
the only object of desire now.

Outside the winter light of late afternoon
reflects body heat in a burn of pale rose,
but I don't care about connection to sky
or position of the sun –
only a promise of cool sheets.

I think of Mother, the epidemic of 1918;
the doctor came, announced as he left –
    *The boy will be okay, but*
    *I don't know about the girl –*
how rage made her well again.

# Winter Solstice

Too soon to note
the sun's new slant —
temperatures slide,
zero minus twenty;
hearts beat not quite in rhythm.

Hunting season done,
hungry deer stop
at the edge of a pond
scarred by skate blades.

In the Green Mountain tea room,
a woman in a white shawl
spreads marmalade on toast,
peers through latticed windows.

Upstairs, four-poster beds
stand empty for the holiday,
patchwork quilts
folded in triangles.

On the Common,
children spread their arms,
carve angel wings
in last night's snow.

Conversation suspends
like icicles from the eaves.
We pass through this town,
do not speak of our solitude.

# New Year's Eve

under cover of dark, a year slips away
in vapor of drizzle and champagne

a palindrome of a year
ends no better than it began

war is the winter offering
weaponry the new catechism

the language of armed conflict pelts
us like drops of freezing rain

*Hellfire missile, Apache gunship,*
*bomb, target, firepower*

the Bethlehem of carols
lies hushed, under siege

we children of the Sixties
sort through our own deaths

remember this kind of year,
this drama of dread

## Twelfth Night

The Christmas tree is down,
dragged to the alley, and
the tabby cat, who liked
to sleep under the tree, is dead.

Red, blue, green ornaments of glass
and the tiny musical instruments
that cannot be played – cello, flute,
French horn, piano, balalaika –

are wrapped in tissue, packed
in a box marked *fragile*,
together with the cardinal,
goldfinch, snowy owl, white

dove and ceramic angel,
carried to the top of the house,
pushed back on their attic shelf
until the next winter solstice.

Star gazing magi have turned east
after leaving their exotic gifts:
precious metals and aromatic resins.
We shelve new books and sweaters.

On stage, Shakespeare reunites
Sebastian and Viola one more time,
because his own twins
were parted with permanence.

The origins of love cannot be plumbed;
winter breeds its own kind of alone.
The cat is ashes, to be scattered
at vernal equinox, before dogwoods bloom.

# Weather Report

Like diamonds on glass, cold
scratches skin. The wind sings in a harsh key
parables of Northern nights.

Spirits of ice ages hover
on brittle wings, whistle
in waves that hurt human ears.

There is no solace in this cold,
though you wrap yourself
in the wool of ancestors.

You may doze off
in languid dreams of gulf islands,
spring planting, camellias in bloom.

But you are too far from the pull
of equinox; your day will turn hard
on axis of metallic ice.

# Turning Sixty

A day when light equals dark,
I turn sixty
in a Back Bay bed-and-breakfast,
watch as another war unfurls.

This violence beams its own televised light –
eerie green glow of bombs over Baghdad,
sand storms a prism for rose desert sun.
My mouth dry as this vision of dust and death,

I switch off war, taxi across Boston
to line up in awe
before Monet's light on canvas –
brushstrokes explode softly in my brain.

Emboldened by war,
by equinox fever,
I am seized by sudden impulse
to violate museum rules,

to reach out, touch his red poppies,
haystacks, the snow at Argenteuil,
trace a languid water lily, invite
his current of light into my body.

But I suppress the urge,
leave art to celebrate birth,
dine on lobster in ginger and wine,
bread of angels, chocolate bittersweet.

Small comfort there is this year
in the greening of the land,
equality of night and day,
early evening blood sun.

# Vernal Equinox

Father, this anniversary
of my birth and your death
is an odd event on the calendar,
always signals a time of year
when I am in the power of some new love
or other purveyor of magic tricks.

In a race from now to solstice,
daylight lengthens,
and forsythia gives way
to violet, crabapple, azalea,
over-indulged in fuchsia and pink.
Like birth and death, spring
raises impossible expectations.

The surgeon cut your voice away,
and you wrote notes to us
as I write to you now,
decades after the funeral
where the *Ariosa* by Bach
filled the space between us.

The sun has crossed the equator
and moves north
seeking alignment
with northern hemisphere,
as I still seek mine to you.

# Late Snow

Always a surprise,
March snow that burdens
daffodils and early magnolias
with sudden weight,
like a sign in a strange language,

like the photo of mother at sixteen,
corners of her mouth amused
when I lift the tarnished frame
from the attic box of ribbons,
cloth dolls and old coins,

like war in a country
where we used to live,
like your death on my birthday
in the gray pre-light of spring,
just before the snow.

# Spring Cleansing

I wash my hair
with golden seal, cranesbill,
burdock root, buckthorn bark,
elder flowers, slippery elm,
rainwater from Grandmother's
cellar cistern.

This April ritual
cleanses me of
last year's death,
and my winter lover.

Hair still wet, I plant
cilantro, basil, phlox.
From a stone church
on the square, Mozart's
*Vesperae Solennes De Confessore*
filters early evening light.

Tomorrow I sail
to Newfoundland,
Atlantic time,
longer days,
an uncommon love.

## Salmon Run

How efficient these Chinook, Sockeye, Coho.
Hatched after parents die,
young salmon suffer no separation anxiety,
no mal effects of abandonment;
they just know when it's time
to swim downstream, silvery gills
alert to the lure of salt water.

After a year or three of ocean life –
evading whales, larger fish, fishermen,
they are seized by impulse
       to reproduce and die.
Memory of the sweet smell
of the spawning ground
drives the upstream swim –
       better than love or sex.

In freshwater, they glisten, jump, leapfrog,
not discouraged by the long voyage,
rapids and waterfalls, the unknown:
       whether death is final
       or the soul lives on.

No time to feed,
they consume their own insides,
fueled by an end of life ecstasy
that leads straight to the birthplace.
They know when to stop:
females dig gravelly wombs
for a few thousand eggs,

males release all their sperm.
Passion spent, flesh empty,
suspended in familiar waters,
they droop, wait
for bald eagles and bears.

## Athabasca

Conceived in the snows
of the Pleistocene,
metamorphosed crystals,
set in motion
by their own weight,
sculptured and ravished
mountains, moved rock, silt, clay,
in each slow rasp
of advance and retreat.

We mark time in decades;
the ice measures millennia
of cirque carvings on mountainsides;
limestone, dolomite dissolved;
moraines of rocks
plucked, moved, abandoned;
jade lakes gouged and fed
by ancient waters
of englacial streams.

An old woman stoops
to touch the glacial tongue;
a child cups hands
in a meltwater rivulet cascading
toward a polished blue mill hole,
brings her hands to her lips,
drinks from an ice age.

# The Burren

More like a moon than earth,
Stark limestone landscape,
Glacier gouged and scraped.
A portal tomb holds balance,
As it has for six thousand years,
Over bones of a people who did not know
They were the early act of an Irish saga;
Or that cutting all the trees would erode
The soil that sustained them, down
To this slippery rock where only tough
Wildflowers survive in the fissures; or
How differing visions of God would blight
This island forever.  We tiptoe gingerly.

# Nebulae

Inuit watch the world melt
beneath their feet,
while farther south sandbars
wash away, deltas disappear.

Astronomers feel the pulse
of a star collapsed,
its nebula an apparition,
like a dead lover's ghost.

We measure time by the light
of another doomed star,
and after sixty or so cycles
around the sun, the body

prods with its temporal nature,
as the mind tries to wrap itself
around this life's limits,
slippery as jellyfish.

Carol Jennings grew up in the rolling hills of western New York, attended The College of Wooster, graduated from NYU, lived for more than a decade in New York City, and now resides in Washington DC. In New York, she worked at both the United Nations and the American Civil Liberties Union before earning a J.D. from the NYU School of Law. For much of her legal career, she served in the Federal Trade Commission's Bureau of Consumer Protection. She is author of an article on "The Woman Poet," published in *The New York Quarterly* in 1972, and also served on the editorial staff of *NYQ* during the early years of its publication. Her poems have appeared in a number of journals, including *The New York Quarterly, Chautauqua, The Broadkill Review, Innisfree Poetry Journal, Beltway Poetry Quarterly, Oberon, Potomac Review,* and *Medical Literary Messenger*, as well as three anthologies. Two of her poems have won awards at The Chautauqua Institution, where she spends time each summer. She is now retired and devotes her time to poetry and the piano. Visit her website at http:://www.carol-jennings.com.

www.ingramcontent.com/pod-product-compliance
Lightning Source LLC
Chambersburg PA
CBHW020806160426
43192CB00006B/456